transforming lives

TURNING UGANDA'S FORGOTTEN CHILDREN INTO LEADERS

stephen shames

Foreword by Pete Norman

Star Bright Books
New York

LIFE IN UGANDA

Nestled in the middle of Africa and straddling the equator, Uganda is similar in size to the state of Oregon and has a population of about 32 million—slightly less than California. But there the similarities end. The people of Uganda are dying. A baby born in Uganda is ten times more likely to die before its first birthday than an infant in the United States.

For many Ugandans, the future is too far away to dream about and the struggle to survive is very real. Like a lot of Africa, families in Uganda are large and extended and virtually every family is affected by poverty, HIV/AIDS, and brutal war. Decades of civil war have damaged this country and the greatest fear is the rebels—the Lord's Resistance Army (LRA), led by Joseph Kony.

The civil war on the northern border of the country left 90% of the region's population internally displaced. The rebel soldiers mutilated and killed innocent men, women, and children. Hands, ears, noses, and lips were cut off by rebel soldiers. The terrified rural villagers were forced to give the rebels food and shelter and not help government troops trying to crush the civil war.

Food was not the only commodity the rebels stole. As many as 20,000 children were abducted. If parents weren't killed, they watched helplessly as their children were led away, never to be seen again. Claiming to have black magic powers, rebel leaders stopped many children from escaping simply by threatening supernatural retribution.

Boys and girls were forced to carry stolen weapons and supplies for the rebels, and were also forced to attack other children who tried to escape. Many of the stolen boys were forced to fight against government troops. They were given machetes (known as pangas), wooden clubs, and even rifles, and these child soldiers were forced to maim and kill during raids. Once "bloodied," the rebels figured the child soldiers would be easier to control. Many of these former child soldiers still have memories of forced atrocities that have left them with recurring nightmares and guilt.

Countless Ugandan children have been orphaned by war and HIV/AIDS. Like many countries, rich and poor, Uganda has no major support system when someone gets sick or injured. Hospitals are basic and few and far between. There is no welfare system, and family members are expected to provide for each other.

When children are left without parents, they are forced to fend for themselves. Like many of the children in this book, it is common for an older child to look after younger siblings, and their dream of school becomes distant on the list of priorities.

The stories in this book tell of children who have had horrendous experiences, and yet their desire to excel has persisted. Many have made promises of helping their country and our planet. They are the hope for the future of Uganda.

—Pete Norman

Gulu. Night commuters.
Thousands of children
walk miles every day to
avoid being abducted.

L.E.A.D UGANDA

"When I lost my father I thought that was the end of my story, but I am happy you brought my tears into great happiness."

—Wasswa, L.E.A.D Uganda student

While on assignment in Uganda doing a story on AIDS, I photographed the funeral of a woman who had died leaving behind five orphans. I formed a special relationship with Sarah, the youngest, who calls me "Dad." I paid for Sarah's family, as well as a dozen other orphans from the village, to attend the best primary and secondary schools.

By 2004, this evolved into a leadership program called L.E.A.D Uganda. Five years later, the lives of 70+ children, including Sarah, have been transformed. These AIDS orphans, refugees, former child soldiers, street kids, and child laborers are excelling in school. Twenty maintain "A" averages, and 13 received top grades on their national exams. One has been accepted by the African Leadership Academy in South Africa, one of Africa's best schools. Six attend university, and of these, three received full scholarships. Fourteen hold leadership positions at their schools.

While many nonprofit organizations in Africa pay school fees for children, L.E.A.D Uganda is unique in its emphasis on training leaders. We send our scholars to the best boarding schools and give them everything they need to succeed, including leadership workshops and emotional support. We arm former child soldiers with the 21st-century skills necessary to lead their country into the future. We give child laborers and young people in refugee camps a voice. We help girls stay in school so they aren't forced to marry at an early age. Education transforms lives, builds economic self-sufficiency, and creates hope.

This book is about how AIDS orphans and former child soldiers can become exceptional people—leaders. It is written to honor the millions of young people in Uganda who cling to their dreams even though they are affected by AIDS, war, and poverty. It is also written for *you* because you have the power to help them transform their lives—and change the world.

—Stephen Shames

Opposite page: Rahim and Sarah at the L.E.A.D Uganda office. Sarah's brother, Joseph, peers in through the window.

Above: Ojok in Amida IDP Camp. **Left:** Lira. 12-year-old Ojok with Major Okot Ayol Silvio at a reunion between former LRA commanders and child soldiers after Major Okot surrendered. Ojok was Major Okot's bodyguard, who later saved his life when the LRA tried to kill him.

Child Soldiers

OJOK

My parents were killed by rebels when I was a baby. My grandparents looked after me. I was nine years old when the rebels came to our camp. It was 3 a.m. on a Sunday. I was sleeping in a hut with friends. My grandparents and sister were in a different part of the camp. I was only partly dressed when the rebels led me away. I was tied by rope in a line—six boys, seven girls, five women, and one big man—as we marched into the bush.

The rebels had managed to raid the camp because the guards were sleeping. My grandmother discovered I was missing when she came to get me in the morning. She alerted the army commander and about 16 soldiers tracked us in the bush. We had walked about four miles carrying six bags of grain from the camp to a river. When the soldiers arrived, a gun battle started and although we were tied together, we ran away. After the battle, the rebels recaptured us. They split us between two rebel commanders. I was taken by one who noticed I was very strong. He liked how I answered questions so he made me a bodyguard. I had to protect him and his wife. She was only 15.

The rebels taught me to use, clean, and strip weapons. The rebels do evil things. They mutilate people and watch them die. They force boy soldiers to kill and rape. I still have nightmares about the nine people I was forced to kill. I was only ten years old when I killed the first one. You kill or the rebels kill you. I hope people understand that I was forced to do evil.

Sometimes I would be told to take a person into the bush and kill them. I would take them far away and tell them, "Run away now, before I kill you." They would hardly believe it and then thank me. I would shoot in the ground to make it sound as if I had killed them. I didn't want to kill old people because that would be like killing my grandmother.

I had been in the bush for two years when an army helicopter came after us. The commander gave me a rocket-propelled grenade. I was shaking and tried to shoot the helicopter but couldn't hit it. The helicopter crew chased after me and shot me.

I am very lucky to be alive. The abducted child soldiers took me to a place in the bush that the rebels used to look after their injured and pregnant women. It wasn't a hospital, just huts. No one really cares for you there. I stayed there for two months. I was lucky no bones were broken.

I went back to the rebels and right away the leader gave me a gun. One day, as we crossed a big dirt road, I pretended to be sick and said I needed to go to the bathroom—in the bush you just dig a hole. I hid and the rebels moved on. I waited an hour before backtracking to the road. I didn't know where it led, but I used my bush skills—knowing the sun rises in the east and sets in the west—and followed it. For about three months I followed the road, sleeping under trees, eating wild food and surviving on hardly any water. I was alone in the remote bush in Sudan. Some days all I ate was a single mango. I was 12 years old.

One morning I saw soldiers. I hid my gun and uniform and moved further into the bush to get away from the gun. The soldiers pointed their rifles at me when I came out of the bush near their barracks. They interrogated me, and I explained how I had escaped from the rebels. I took them to where I had hidden my gun, uniform, bullets, and bag of grenades. I had felt so protected when I had a gun, and now I had to hand it to them. Giving my weapons to the soldiers was a sign of my final surrender.

The soldiers took care of me. I was sent to a center for ex-child soldiers. That is when I met Steve Shames. He took me back to my home district. The roads are dangerous because of the rebels, so we went in a little airplane to the IDP (Internally Displaced Person) camp. My sister was there and when I got off the plane she ran to tell my grandmother that I was alive. My grandmother fainted when she heard the news.

Steve Shames asked me if I wanted to study and of course I said, "Yes." When I first joined L.E.A.D Uganda, my grades were not so good, but now I am among the top 18 in my class—the class has 95 students in it. I love learning about science. Social studies and English are my favorite. I like L.E.A.D Uganda because they are doing a job I want to continue with. They want to make a better future for us. By being educated, we will be prepared to help others who are not so fortunate. The people in the north are so poor and the education level so low that schooling is very, very basic. My grandmother was a nurse and my grandfather was an engineer. I want to be a doctor and help other children everywhere I can—here in Kampala or in the north. I want to help children go to school.

When I told L.E.A.D Uganda about my past, I didn't want to tell them that I killed people. It took a year before I told. That was two years ago and I am glad I was brave enough to tell my history. I am healing.

OLWENY

Ever since I was born, there have been troubles in the north with rebels. My parents named me Olweny, which means "during conflict."

When the rebels attacked, my mom stayed in our hut while we all escaped into the bush with my father. We slept all night in the bush and went back to our compound in the morning. As we approached, I saw my mother lying next to our hut, dead. I was only seven but my pain was not over. The rebels came again and killed my father. Later, I was abducted.

One day when we crossed the border from Sudan, seven young abducted children asked a guard to let them rest, but instead, he killed them. Two of them were my best friends. Now I look at things differently from other children.

I missed four years of school. The first year back at school was difficult because I had forgotten almost everything. But in ninth grade everything became better because I studied hard. Because I was older than the other students, some teased me; they called me the "dad" of the class.

I now have a certificate in video production. I work for a non-governmental organization teaching video and art to children affected by war. I also shoot video for a television station in Gulu.

I don't have any photographs of my parents, so I draw them. If my parents were alive now and saw me—my dad, who was a craftsman and made drums—would be smiling happily for me.

Opposite page: Gulu. Olweny and friend. Right: Drawings by Olweny. (top): Rebels ask woman where her children are. (center): Olweny's mother after she was killed. (bottom): Children pray in school.

RONALD

One day when I was walking to get water, I saw rebels coming, so I started to run. One of them chased me and yelled, "Boy, don't run. I will shoot you if you run." I froze. He tied my hands behind my back and made me follow him. The rebels made me lie down in the dirt with my hands behind my back and put a heavy log on the back of my neck. It was difficult to breathe. Then they hit me about 30 times with a big stick.

They forced me to get up and we walked many miles before stopping at a camp. A boy gave me a little cooked maize to eat. As punishment, the rebels did not give me food for four days. After four days I could not walk. Even so, they gave me a 20-liter can to get water from the well. It was so heavy it fell off my head and burst. The rebels whacked me 20 times with a cane and said I would not get food for another two days. Then they gave me another can and said, "If this one bursts we will kill you." I dared not carry it on my head.

The rebel leader, Joseph Kony, was always there with his gun, watching and ready to kill any of us. He sent me with 80 other boys for "registration." "We don't have books or pens for registration, instead we will cane you with a hot panga." The rebels told us to bend over; then they slapped us four times on our backs with the hot metal panga. They said the panga had magical powers and it would save us. Then they hit us many times on the buttocks with a cane. The rebels gave us oil from a witch doctor to treat the wounds. We couldn't sleep on our backs for a week because it was so painful.

A month later the rebels trained us to shoot. We each got a rifle and four bullets. They warned us, "If you miss the target you will get caned 20 times." I had never fired a gun before. I missed the target twice so I was hit 40 times on my back. After that they taught us how to operate and clean a gun, and how to ambush. We were given dirty, bloodstained uniforms from Ugandan soldiers who had been killed.

The rebels also took one of my brothers. I gave him food but they said, "Before you feed him you have to mistreat him." I beat him and then gave him food. I did that for a week. Then they separated us because they thought we would escape together. They did not let me say goodbye. I don't know if he is still alive.

Later, I was with the rebels when they raided my village. They made my family get out of their hut. One of the rebels told me to kill my father. You can't say no to the rebels or they just kill you, but I said, "Kill me. I will not kill this man." Another boy with a panga started to hack my father to pieces. My mother was screaming. The rebels told my mother to put his body in the hut. I felt like shooting the rebels. I wanted to scream but kept quiet because I didn't want the rebels to kill us and everyone else in the village. For a long time I had dreams about my parents' faces. I asked the boy who killed my father why he did it. He said it was because the rebels ordered him to "kill that dog." One week after he killed my father I turned the gun on him and pulled the trigger. When you are fighting in the bush you can kill people and no one will know. The rebels can't overthrow the government, so they terrorize the people instead.

Ronald studying inside his family's hut in Pader IDP Camp.

Above: The Road to Pader IDP Camp. Ronald and Ongom ride home from school guarded by soldiers as they pass through territory where rebels are active.
Left: Pader IDP Camp. Ronald sleeps outside so he can hear rebels approaching and because he fears fires, which are frequent in the camps.

Kony had an escort of four boys. He liked me, so I was one of them. As an escort I was treated better. Kony got the best food and we ate what he had. For three years I was with Kony and was not afraid of him. I had my gun and felt strong. Sometimes Kony was very funny, but he could very easily have killed me.

The rebels forced us to kill. I killed ten people. If I could talk to their families, I would say, "I am sorry." When I was with the rebels I didn't have nightmares about my actions, but away from them, I do. When I dream I can see a real person's face screaming, "No, no, no." I will never forget those things, but I hope I heal.

During a battle against government forces I was shot near my right wrist. I fell and a government soldier found me. He took me to the government hospital where I stayed for two months. The wound on my arm wouldn't heal. The doctor said, "The only thing we can do is cut your arm off to save your life." I was not happy about losing my arm but maybe it is punishment for what I had to do.

I was living in Pader when Steve Shames of L.E.A.D Uganda found me. He talked to my mom about going to Kampala to study. My mom and I were very happy. I wanted to study so much. Now, I go to high school. The teachers are good but they don't feed us well. I play basketball and football there.

Without L.E.A.D Uganda, I would be dead. With only one arm I would be useless in a village—you can't dig and no one will look after you. I was right-handed before they amputated my arm. I am still learning to write with my left hand. My father would be proud of me if he were alive. I know my mother is.

My life has changed so much because of L.E.A.D Uganda. They bought me clothes and my very first pair of shoes. I went to the Albert Einstein Medical Center in America for a prosthetic arm with two attachments— a hand and a hook. The doctor who helped me, Dr. Alberto Esquenazi, has only one arm too. It was good meeting someone who understood my situation. Now I have another arm so I don't have to ask friends to wash my clothes. Some people in my village have never seen Kampala and they have good arms and legs. I have seen the other side of the world with only one good arm.

In ten years I hope to be educated and married. I want to be a lawyer and do the work that L.E.A.D Uganda does. I want to help orphaned children and to construct boreholes in the villages so people don't have to walk long distances for water.

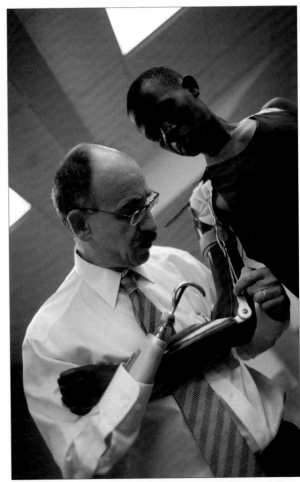

Philadelphia. Dr. Esquenazi adjusts Ronald's prosthetic arm.

AIDS Orphans

SARAH

Iwas born in a small village. I don't remember my mom or dad because they died from AIDS before my first birthday. Life was hard in my village. My sister Rose took care of me. She would grow food in our garden, wash our clothes, and try to go to school. We did not have enough food. An aunt would sometimes give us money to buy food. When I was two years old, Rose went away to boarding school, so my seven-year-old sister Sanyu had to look after my two brothers and me.

I had to leave school early each day with my older brother Joseph so he could cook. We would save some food for Sanyu to eat when she came home from school. Every day was the same struggle. I would fetch water and Joseph would cook. The well was about four or five miles round trip. I carried a two-gallon container on my head. It was heavy so I only filled it halfway.

The villagers felt sorry for us. Sometimes when Sanyu was at school the neighbors gave me food. When I grow up I would like to help them.

My life now is so different. The school I go to is much better than the one in my village. I wear clean clothes and I don't have to walk long distances. I have food and water here. I just have to read and study. I want to do well in primary school so I can go to Seeta High School. Seeta is where Sanyu goes. Sometimes I wish she were still in primary school with me.

There are 53 girls in my dormitory. Our days are really long. We wake up at 5 a.m. The matron hits the door and calls, "Wake up, it's time. Go and bathe." We wash with sponges and clean our teeth. We have to wait in line to use the toilets. Sometimes there's no toilet paper so we have to use paper from a notebook. We don't have flushing toilets at school or at home. We have to squat above a hole.

After bathing we make our beds and clean the dorm. Then we have porridge in the dining hall. Our first lesson is at 7 a.m. We have a break at 10 a.m. for one hour, and classes end at 4 p.m. After school I can have a sponge bath and change into my after-school uniform. Then we can play. Every night we have supper at 7 p.m. Once a month we get haircuts. It is nice to have short hair when it is hot, and it stops lice.

We have classes six days a week. On Sundays we sleep late and get up at 7 a.m. We go to church, and then we can spend the day playing. My favorite foods are muceere [rice] and enkoko [chicken], which we only get on Sunday. I also like matooke [steamed plantain]. I love obushera, a drink made out of millet. The worst thing about school is they put less sugar in our porridge and less salt in the food.

Above: Kalungi Village, Rakai. Sarah rides on her brother Frank's back. **Right:** Relatives at the wake for Nakawesi Pasikazia who died of AIDS, leaving five children: Rose, Frank, Sanyu, Joseph, and Sarah.

L.E.A.D Uganda helped me learn English. It is hard to learn, but Luganda, my language, is hard too. Teachers make us speak English. If they hear us speak Luganda or if you have poor handwriting, they make you "carry the bone." The bone is the leg of a dog, the size of your palm. It is on a string, so you can put it over someone's neck. One day I was in a hurry to leave class and wrote badly, so I had to carry the bone. I then found a boy speaking Luganda and I put it on him. If you are the last one wearing the bone you get caned, so it is best not to have it!

When I went to America with other L.E.A.D students, it was so cold I could ice skate on the frozen water. That was the first time I saw snow. It was on the ground and on the cars. We made snowballs and threw them at each other.

When I came home to Uganda, I tried to explain what snow was like to my best friend, Shirat, but it is hard to explain to someone who has never seen it. Ice skating was the best thing in America. It was such fun falling down. It didn't hurt, and it was just for laughs. I also remember seeing fish when I was in America but they weren't in a lake, they were in water in a glass tank. But the thing I didn't like in America was carrot cake—because it is not sweet enough for me!

I honor the memory of my parents by doing well in school. I came second in my class in the first term, but it was not good enough for me. I wanted to be first because I want to be the best for L.E.A.D Uganda. So I studied really hard, and was first in my class last term. I want to be a leader and help the children of Uganda. A leader has to learn. Being a leader is partly about being humble, but it is also about teaching others what to do. I want to be a headmistress—a principal. We call our teachers "Mama." I want to be a mama to many. I want to help children and maybe one day take some of them to America and show them the things I saw. I want to take care of them just like L.E.A.D Uganda has helped me. If I were still in my village I wouldn't have these options. My life was changed—it was transformed all because I was given the chance to have a good education.

Opposite page: Sarah and her best friend, Shirat, at Budo Junior School. Above (right): Sarah on her first day in the first grade.

SANYU

If I weren't in L.E.A.D Uganda, I wouldn't be in school. I would be like a mother, looking after my sister and brother. I would be stuck in the village fetching water, digging for food, and collecting firewood for the rest of my life. Jobs are hard to get and there are so many people living on the streets in our country. I'm lucky to get a second chance. Now our family won't be on those streets.

There are a lot of children at my school from rich families and so it is easy to feel out of place. It is embarrassing when kids ask about my parents, so I try to seem too busy to answer. This pushes me to study more. I am in the top ten in my class of 97 students, and I applied to become one of the elected leaders at school.

I want to become a doctor to treat people's diseases. When you are a doctor you advise others and become a model for how people should live. Doctors can pass on the message about the danger of AIDS. The older generation did not know about AIDS. This is why so many people, like my parents, died. When I become a doctor, I will look after Uganda's children.

Opposite page: Sanyu studying. **Below:** Sanyu fetching water at school.

WASSWA

I grew up in a poor family, and I didn't want my children to grow up the same way. I really wanted to be a photographer and computer wizard when I grew up, but it wasn't easy. First off, I had no electricity at home, I didn't have a computer, and I didn't have a camera. I used L.E.A.D Uganda's cameras and computers. I just graduated with a certificate in video and photography, and I work for L.E.A.D Uganda. I shoot videos and take photographs for their website and fundraising efforts.

I always think about what makes the perfect photo. I want the picture to explain. If I shoot 100 photos then it is possible just one is good enough to show the world. If I can make money from my pictures, I will set up a small business for my mom. She has suffered a lot for us. Then I will help other kids.

I would love to be a leader for the young people of Uganda. The headmaster and the head teacher at my school asked me if I wanted to be a head boy. "If you do, start campaigning now," they said. I gave my first public speech ever. Everyone clapped. I won the vote. I don't know how big L.E.A.D Uganda will grow, but I want to help pay school fees for children and invest in their future. When I die, maybe they will remember that Wasswa Charles was one of the first who was helped, and he in return helped others.

AIDS, AIDS. AIDS
by Wasswa Charles Setala

I

AIDS, a killer.
AIDS, AIDS. AIDS.
AIDS, a monster
Oh, AIDS, a thief.
You have taken our parents.
And made us orphans.
You have taken away the manpower.
Oh, What a monster you are!
You have stolen the newborn babies,
Who are innocent.
You have stolen our guardians.
What a thief you are!
Oh, AIDS,
You sting like a bee.
You are like a scorching sunshine in the desert.
You are the killer.
I hate you!

II

Your name is Mr. AIDS.
You are proud of it.
You regard yourself as the strongest on the Earth.
I think you are still young.
You are an economist because you have
Reduced the world population and alleviate the
Problem of scarcity.
And work against fellow scientists.
You don't specialize in any kind of people.
You crush the doctors,
Lawyers, teachers,
Reverends, magistrates,
And even, old people.
You save the children by killing them
While they are still young.
You killed my parents.
You worked hard to get rid of them.
And I will work hard to get rid of you.
Be careful because I am planning for you.

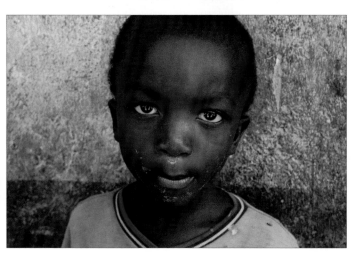

Opposite page: Kampala. Wasswa with a camera. Top: Gulu. Wasswa filming while Ocen interviews a night commuter. Center & bottom: Photos taken by Wasswa.

MADINA

I was 12 when my mom and dad died of AIDS. Seventy percent of the children in our village are orphans like me. As the eldest child in my family, I had to grow food to feed my brothers and sisters.

I started living with my grandparents when I was in sixth grade. My grandfather told me, "I don't have enough money for you to go to high school. You are a girl, so you have to stop school and get married." Just when I was about to stop going to school, I found out that L.E.A.D Uganda was paying school fees for my friend, Sarah, and her sister, Sanyu. L.E.A.D Uganda spoke with my grandfather, who allowed me to join the program. He was very happy that I would be able to remain in school.

I traveled to Kampala for school, and I didn't know any English. I had to repeat a year, but then I started to do well. My English improved and I ended up getting an A+ in that class! English, science, social studies, and math are my favorite subjects. I am among the top ten students in my class of 94. My classmates are very competitive, which encourages me to do even better.

My hope is that I will be able to help others in 20 years. I want to be successful in my job and help orphans, just like I have been helped.

Madina in class.
Opposite page:
Budo Junior School.
Madina with her best
friend, Sanyu.

HILDA

I am deputy head girl at the best high school in Uganda. This is a big achievement for me considering where I come from. My father died the year after I was born and my mother is HIV positive. She had to raise six children—including two of her sister's—while coping with her own possible death. But she struggled on.

Mom had no job. She earned a little money making red AIDS ribbons and beading bracelets for an AIDS organization that uses drama to educate people. But the money she earned wasn't enough to support us and we often went to bed with empty stomachs.

I wanted to lift my family out of poverty. I asked my mother to show me how to make the ribbons and bracelets. I organized my sisters and brothers to make ribbons and bracelets, and I sold them to delegates attending AIDS conferences. This family business helped us get food and allowed my siblings and me to go back to primary school. In addition, it boosted my self-confidence.

Even with our small business, there was not enough money to pay my high school fees. I was going to drop out after seventh grade, but then I heard what L.E.A.D Uganda was doing for children in our country. They checked my school records and accepted me into the program, as I was the best in my class.

L.E.A.D Uganda allowed me to shine. I never imagined I would find myself at the best school in the country—let alone be deputy head girl. A lot of rich families send their children to my school. They are the cream of Uganda—children of government ministers, business people, and other top families. Although I keep in mind where I come from, I do not allow my past to keep me down.

I love this school. It is inspirational. The teachers encourage me to excel. I am self-driven. I don't wait for the school bell to start work. We are supposed to be up at five in the morning but I get up earlier. Similarly, I try to get to class before it starts. I love math. My other favorites are chemistry, biology, and physics. I want to study and be successful.

Leadership is really needed in this country. This is why I have been encouraged to develop my leadership skills at school. I am senior deputy head girl even though I am only in 11th grade. I love my life. My mother is proud of me.

My goal is to be a neurosurgeon. I will create jobs by building my own hospital. I will probably have to leave Uganda to study because we lack facilities. But I don't think that is a bad thing. I will gain knowledge, come back as a neurosurgeon, and use my skills to help reduce suffering in my country.

Opposite page: Kampala. Hilda prepares food. **Right:** Hilda fetches water.

Life in the Camps

ONGOM

Ever since the war started people in northern Uganda have been living in IDP camps. They lack water and food. Each year, more than 2,000 children can't study because their parents do not have money for school fees and they fear being abducted at school.

One day on my way to school I was abducted. There were 45 rebels. I was scared when I saw them holding guns. I thought they would kill me.

I managed to escape. When I finally returned home, I found my father had died and my mother was engaged to another man. I decided to stay with my grandmother in Pader IDP Camp. I slept outside because it was hot in the hut and I feared fires. I attended a primary school with 52 other students. We had no books, no desks, and no chalkboard. Soldiers escorted us to and from school. My grandmother couldn't afford to buy kerosene for our lamp. Without light, studying in the evenings was impossible.

I stayed in the camp for two years until L.E.A.D Uganda put me into King's College Budo, Uganda's best secondary school. I work hard in order to have a better life.

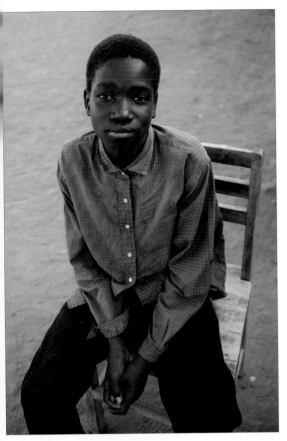

NOKRACH

My dad was killed by rebels when I was young. My mom didn't cry—she just hugged me.

The rebels raid day and night and take the boys they want. I remember the first time they attacked. I was just seven years old. They tore off our clothes and beat us with big sticks. I saw people chopped to death with a panga. The rebels made our village watch as they cooked the bodies in three huge pots, saying, "If we ever see you support the soldiers we will do the same to you." Thankfully, they didn't make us eat the bodies. I have nightmares about the killings.

I was abducted for eight months. I had to carry things the rebels stole. I didn't kill anyone but I had to beat people when the rebels raided villages. I felt sorry when I saw people killed. I saw the rebels heat a panga until it was red-hot and use it to beat boys. The boys would scream and fall down in pain.

I was scared of the rebel leader, Kony, but after a week I got used to him. When the rebels sent me to get firewood, I ran away. If they had found me, they would have killed me.

If I were still in the village, I'd have been abducted again. I have seen a lot that children shouldn't see. L.E.A.D Uganda interviewed me, and when they heard my story, they sent me to school. At first I couldn't speak English or the local language, Luganda, although I could understand it. Now I speak three languages. I am learning French. It will help when I visit other countries.

I want to be a doctor or an engineer so I can be a leader and address the problems we have in our country. One of the worst things affecting Africa is malaria. I want to help. I hope I will be able to encourage kids, raise their quality of life, and help them succeed. I can't tell my dad about my life, but my mom is proud of me.

Opposite page: Pader IDP Camp. Primary school classroom. **Above (top):** Ongom. (bottom): Nokrach.

AMOS

My dad was killed by the rebels in 2002. He had gone to our garden to dig when he was shot. I saw him afterwards, lying there. My mom, Lakot Betty, was crying and screaming. Up until that point we were still living in our village, but then we moved to Amida IDP camp for safety.

Four years later I came to Kampala to study. I love to study. My local language is Acholi. At school my favorite subject is English, and I love science. It might seem strange but there is nothing I hate about school. I love it all. I am very lucky L.E.A.D Uganda pays my school fees and all the other costs that come with school.

I want to be a doctor to help people. This is something my mother and my sisters will be proud of. Mom is already proud of what I have achieved. I am first in my class. I go home for vacation three times a year. The eight-hour journey home is long and difficult, but it is so good to see my mom there. She hugs me so hard.

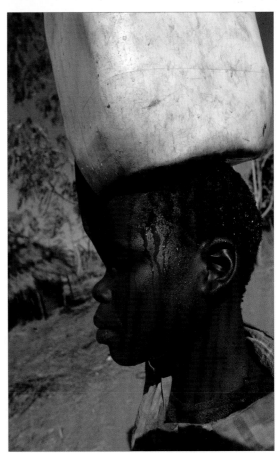

Opposite page: Pader IDP Camp.
Getting water from a hole in the ground.
Above and right: Amida IDP Camp,
Kitgum. Amos pumps and carries water.

– 31 –

Child Laborers

KATONGOLE

When I was younger, I worked in a quarry, breaking rocks into pebbles. I used a hammer that I made myself by tying a rock to a stick. I made only 1500 shillings [73¢] a day so I couldn't afford to go to school full-time. I broke rocks until I had money for my school supplies, shoes, and uniform. I started school when the others were taking their midterms, but I still managed to be top in my class.

When Steve saw my school results he told me he would get me into the best school. He kept his promise, and I am now the happiest man on the planet because I am going to be a pharmacist!

I was awarded a complete scholarship from the Government of Uganda to study pharmacy in September. When I graduate, I, a former quarry boy, will enter a highly respected and well paid profession.

More important, I will be able to help my country, which suffers from a shortage of pharmacists. [According to the Pharmaceutical Society of Uganda, there are only 350 registered pharmacists in the country, expected to serve 30 million people.]

Pharmacy is more than just counting pills. The pharmacist's role in society is to promote the well-being of his patients. It is a trustworthy occupation that reaches into almost all aspects of medicine and healthcare. I am indeed happy to reach this point in life, because now I am viewed as important by my nation and by my family.

Left: Kampala. Katongole splitting rocks into pebbles at a rock quarry. Opposite page: Kampala. Katongole reading outside his home. He graduated from high school with top honors.

Naggalama High School.
Ntege in class.

NTEGE

When I was in primary school, I had to work part-time in a rock quarry, carrying stones. If I hadn't worked, we wouldn't have had enough money for food. I earned 100,000 shillings [$52] for a month's work.

I wanted to study and though I missed so much school, I still got one of the best grades in the country on my Primary Leaving Examination. But my family could not afford to send me to high school, so I had to forget about studying.

My headmistress told my story to the newspaper, and Steve Shames read about me. He came to the quarry and to my home. L.E.A.D Uganda helped me attend high school at Naggalama. I did so well I transferred to Namugongo, the top high school. Then I was encouraged to apply to the African Leadership Academy (ALA). I didn't know anything about it, so I researched it at an internet café. I thought, "If I go there, I can be a leader in the country." There were more than 1,700 applications from Africa so it was tough to get in. Ninety-six students from Uganda applied.

I was selected to go to the finalist's weekend. We took exams in English, math, and literature, and were asked about our background. We had to debate with each other. I made a strong case for good governance. There was a test in which we described our future through the use of an object. I want to be a doctor so I described myself as a syringe. I was asked questions about the future of Africa and the world. They asked who was most inspiring in Africa. I chose Dr. Rhokaya Gueye of Senegal. She is a doctor who built a hospital for women in Senegal. She loves her country and Africa.

The staff at L.E.A.D Uganda asked me if I thought I would pass the exams. Leaders are supposed be decisive, so I said, "Yes." I did not quiver, but in my heart I was scared. I was happy when the results were announced because I was one of only 106 students from all of Africa to be admitted. Only three were from Uganda. When I graduate from ALA I will apply to the best universities in America or England. But I have a passion for Africa. After my studies, I will return to work in Uganda.

Africa has a lot of problems—but they can be solved. The worst problem is corruption of officials. It is everywhere. Disease is also a problem. If you are sick, you might end up in a hospital. If you have money, you will be treated. If not, you will be ignored. Many people in villages die of ill-nesses because the clinics are far away and badly equipped. I will never forget the time my mother was sick. We could not take her to the hospital because we had no money. We used herbs to treat her. That experience made me want to become a doctor so I could help the poor.

The academy has been a great place for me to learn how to lead across cultures. Margaret Mead said, "Never doubt that a small group of thoughtful, committed citizens can change the world. Indeed it is the only thing that ever has." Living in this community of young, talented Africans who share the same love for our continent has made me realize the future of Africa lies in our hands. We are the hope of our ancestors.

I want to be a leader to help people. I want to fight against AIDS. South Africa, where I am going to the academy, has the highest rate of AIDS in Africa. It is not immune to AIDS, even though it is the richest country. Tuberculosis, hepatitis, and other killer diseases all need to be attacked. I feel it is my job to help get rid of these diseases. I want to be the change I want to see in Africa.

Students Who Help

"I am a recent graduate of the Haverford School in Philadelphia. Through L.E.A.D Uganda, my school was paired with Ocen. We raised the money for Ocen's school fees. He wrote letters which were shared with the student body. Hearing from Ocen personally strengthened our relationship with him. That summer I made a trip to Uganda and visited Ocen's school. He seemed shy at first but quickly opened up. We talked about our lives as students and our respective schools and soon realized we had more in common than we would have expected. I brought him a shirt from Haverford and a Philadelphia Eagles cap. I have seen firsthand the difference that a small group of people can make, and the reward that such a relationship brings to all involved regardless of geographic distance."

—*Jeff Kaiser, The Haverford School*

"I'm from the Bronx, New York City. I'm a 19-year-old student in his senior year in high school. I helped my school sponsor [Nokrach] through L.E.A.D Uganda because I couldn't believe that these kids experienced their villages, families, [and] whole countrysides being torn apart over what I still do not fully understand. What I do understand is that every child deserves a chance at life. Bottom line, I'm just a regular American kid who realized that these kids in Uganda deserve a chance that some of my peers and I take for granted. For now I will continue to help as much as I possibly can."

—*Joshua Godoy, A. Schomberg Academy*

Left: L.E.A.D Uganda students Sarah, Rahim, Joseph, and Siyon on Christmas Day. Opposite page: Seven- year-old Victoria takes the entrance exam at Budo Junior School. She was admitted.

Date 19th/08/08· No

Dear Eileen Miller, Gwen Laureen Meitchik, Annie and Katie.
My name is Sarah Nantaayi·I am one of the students
you are supporting by contributing to the LEAD foundation
an concern for the future, the organisation that looks
after me· Thank you very much for your help· Being able
to attend a good school has changed my life· I attend
Kalinabiri primary School, one of the top school of
Uganda· I am in primary three· I sleep in Zebra
Dormitory· My favorite subject is social studies, and my
favorite teacher is Teacher Agoso and she's the class
teacher· I was the first in the class of 94 pupils·
I was at Rakia Rakai district with my sisters and
brothers, and we lost our parents and couldn't go to
school· I was orphaned at a very young age, but now
am glad that I got at a family at concern for the future
who love me and care for me· My favorite things to do
are running, singing, reading storybooks and learning· My
life have changed for a better since I joined concern
for the future· I am studing to become a [   ]
in future· I have made five new friends·
have children? Where do yo live? When ar-
coming to Uganda to see me?

Thank you for sponsoring my education·
                    Nantaayi - Sarah·

- - - - - - - - - - ·⊙· The end - - - - - - - - - -

Gulu. Monica Nankoma,
Director, L.E.A.D Uganda,
at an art workshop run by
L.E.A.D Uganda students
for night commuters.

How You Can Help

L.E.A.D Uganda locates forgotten children with innate talents and molds them into leaders. We give our bright, motivated AIDS orphans, former child soldiers, youth in refugee camps, and underage workers the world-class, 21st-century skills needed to L.E.A.D Africa into the future.

For a small amount of money you can rock the world of a kid in Uganda. Your contribution will enable an AIDS orphan, former child soldier, an abducted girl, or a child laborer to attend the very best primary and secondary school, then go to university. You will help one of our scholars become a leader who will help Uganda, Africa, and all of us. Don't forget that Barack Obama received a scholarship to a top school when he was young. Would he have become President without that help? He has helped the whole world. Our students will do the same.

Sponsor one of our students. Organize a car wash, have a raffle, a bake sale, or a yard sale. Hold a fund-raising dance, movie night, or sports competition.

Talk to your friends and teachers. Talk to your family, your neighbors, your church, synagogue, or mosque. There are many ways to help. Please do something.

Bring hope to the world. It's as easy as that. For more information about how you can help, please go to www.leaduganda.org.

"Please, give more than you can."
—Pastor Brian Moll, Forefront Church

L.E.A.D
UGANDA

This book is dedicated to Emmanuel (left) and Victorious (right), two children who died of AIDS; Andrea Smith for her support and love; the inspirational children in L.E.A.D Uganda, who are my (and our) children; all the wonderful people who give their time and money so our students can achieve their dreams.

Peter Norman's essay is dedicated to his son, Clem, who has a life of hope ahead.

Published in the United States of America by Star Bright Books, Inc., 30-19 48th Avenue, Long Island City, NY 11101.

The name Star Bright Books and the Star Bright Books logo are registered trademarks of Star Bright Books, Inc.
Please visit www.starbrightbooks.com.
For bulk orders, please email orders@starbrightbooks.com

Hardback ISBN-13: 978-1-59572-213-3

Printed in Canada 9 8 7 6 5 4 3 2 1

Library of Congress Cataloging-in-Publication Data

Shames, Stephen.
 Transforming lives : turning Uganda's forgotten children into leaders / Stephen Shames ; foreword by Pete Norman.
  p. cm.
 ISBN 978-1-59572-213-3 (hbk. : alk. paper)
1. Youth in development--Uganda--Juvenile literature. 2. Youth--Uganda--Political activity--Juvenile literature. 3. Leadership--Uganda--Juvenile literature. 4. Orphans--Education--Uganda--Juvenile literature. 5. Child soldiers--Education--Uganda--Juvenile literature. I. Title.
 HQ799.U35S52 2009
 362.73--dc22
                          2009029068

Pete and Steve would like to thank the following people for their assistance with this book and with L.E.A.D Uganda: John Nagenda. Inger-Lise McMillan. Patrick Cline. Anne Aslett, Stephen Crawford, David Furnish/Elton John Aids Foundation. Lili Perski, Leah Karp/Jacob & Malka Goldfarb Foundation. Lynne & Harold Honickman, Kathy Ruyak/Honickman Foundation. Brian & Allison Moll. Jacob Lange & Omotomi Omolulu. Shawn Willis, Joseph & Trisha Virga, Jessica Yaccino, Alexander Morcos, Stacy & Joel Hock, Shawna Tylke, Daniel Upton, Ivan Tirado-Cordero, Yong Kim, all the wonderful people at Forefront Church. Roberta Russo, Claudia Gonzalez, the Pader Field Office staff/UNHCR. Dr. Richard Dawood/Fleet Street Clinic London. Patrick Rogers, Chris Doherty, Simon Perry/People Magazine. Alan Stoga/FLYP Media. Deo Gombya. Monica Nankoma, Stephen Magezi, Lawrence Ibanda, Evelyn Najjuko, Wasswa Charles, Zerina Abdulighani/L.E.A.D Uganda. The moms, guardians, & community partners. David Fenton, Lai Ling Jew, Arelene Troy/Fenton Communications. Loren Solomon, Mary Ellen Gordon, Nabeela Zahid/Solomon Says. Patrice Tanaka, Kendyl Wright, Cassandra Bianco, Pia Mara Finkell/CRT/Tanaka. Alberto & Rosa Esquenazi/Albert Einstein Medical Center. Howard Brand/Allied Orthodics & Prosthetics. Tene Howard & everyone at Global Kids. Marie-Pierre Darneau. Lois Myller. Joe Baio & Anne Griffin. Clare Karabarinde & Martin Netley. Marsha Vernon/A. Schomberg Academy. Jenna Brereton/The Haverford School. Maureen Byrne, Regina Walsh, Mitch Zeman, Mary Tilghman/Talmadge Hill Community Church. St. Peter's Church. Bernadette Bartholmew/Welsh Valley Middle School. Heide Gutman. Management & staff of the Speke Hotel, Kampala. David Ondrick & Elizabeth Herrera. Paula Peters & Jimmy Monack. Dick Demenus/Tekserve. Peter & Jenny Kaufmann. Sherry Chan, Clark Shu, Joshua, Samantha. Jimmy Kolker. Laurent Girrard & Leonara Mahle. Susan & Bob Linsmier. Benny & Patsy Landa. Charles & Ellen Niles, Nicholas O'han/Elizabeth Irwin School, Ellen & Fred Harris, Mark & Kathlene Comaratta, Renee Harbers, Bill Rose/Quail Roost, Michael Lewitton, Georgia & Ned Gian, Bernard Frei, Gwen Lauren Meitchik & Eileen Miller, Annie & Katie. Sharon, Frances & Joseph Bachman, Maria Westman, Patricia & Tom Stewart, Jack Nausbaum, Christine Kim, Mark & Elizabeth Levine, Frances Campbell & Roger Netzer, Frances & Denise Menton, Robert Usdan & Amy Yenkin, Constance Kronn, Ryan Adamson, Rebecca Fabiano, David Moss & Lauren Rosenblum, Krisitan & Gohar Orozco, Dirkan Eguiluz & Cynthia Orozco, Allisen Patel, Frank & Susan Denenberg, Seo Jeong Kim, Heather Rauscher, Deepa Dahal, Karen Weiss, James Staffan, Ian Brinksman/Church in Toronto. Jessica Lutz & Gaurav Butani/Tunic Love. Al & Pamela Bendich, Melanie Coto, William Gillison/Mt. Olive Baptist Church. Charlotte Southern, Jim Nachtwey, Mary Eaton, Arthur Fleischer, Jr., Sherri Posen, John Oller, Kelly Hnatt. Sue & Paul Lotke, Duncan Campbell, Eric Last, Leonard Sussman, Meg Fidler, Mark Reed, Robin Barber, Jan Case, Daniel & Martha Chesluk, Richard Gray & Joanne Donker, Linn Perkins & Stephan Syz, Mandy Woods & John McNeil, Lisa Rasmussen & Burr Nash, William & Ruth Smith, Will Hopkins & Mary K. Baumann, Clifford Chance, Lawrence & Jackie Kamin. Joshua Shames. Steven Kasher & Susan Spungen. Phyllis Stoffman. Mark Stevens. Errol Daniels. Andrea Chalupa. Sarah & Reed Phillips.